Frustrated with yelp!

Erik Devash

Frustrated with yelp!

Copyright © 2013 by Erik Devash

ISBN 978-0-578-12407-0

Table of Contents

Introducing Yelp.com – The Good, the Bad, and the Ugly

Do you wish you could just skip "the whole Yelp thing" altogether? Well, if it doesn't work for the ostrich…

…it's not going to work for you, either. And besides, you're not an ostrich! You're a small businessperson!

So don't bother sticking your head in the sand – Yelp.com will still be there whether or not you choose to face it, and it will still have the potential to either make or break your small business. Trust me, I know all about it. I have been working with small businesses for years, helping them market and promote themselves online. In early 2005, a few months after Yelp.com was established, I started getting calls asking:

"What is Yelp.com? And what's a Yelper!?"

"How do I get more positive Yelp reviews for my business?"

However more recently I'm being asked variations of the same couple questions:

"What do I do about this awful Yelp review!?"

"Why is Yelp filtering my positive reviews and only showing the negative ones!?"

I'm also asked:

"Where the hell did I put my keys? I'm already late for a meeting!"

I can't help you with that last one (check the couch though, always check the couch), but after helping so many folks gain a better understanding of Yelp.com and showing them how to benefit from the site or at least how to minimize the damage it can cause their business, a light bulb finally went off in my head.

"Hey," I thought, "there should be a book about Yelp.com; a resource with all the information businesspeople need about the good, the bad, and the ugly of Yelp!"

But that book didn't exist.
So I wrote it myself.

I can't promise that as soon as you have finished reading this book, you will suddenly get hundreds of five star reviews that will rocket your business to being the internet's very top-rated hamburger stand/hardware store/print shop/dental practice. And I can't promise that reading this book will ensure that you never get another negative Yelp review. Being a great business is your job, and ultimately that's the best way to get good reviews and avoid bad ones.

But, helping you understand why and how people say things about your business, and how you can increase instances of the good and mitigate instances of the bad? *That* I can promise to help you with.

Here is just a taste of what you will better understand when you have finished reading *Frustrated with Yelp?!*:

> • How reviews get onto Yelp.com in the first place, and who is writing them

• Why some businesses seem to get more positive or negative reviews than others

• How the much despised Yelp Filter operates

• How you can deal with negative reviews that are affecting your business

• How you can put Yelp.com to better work for your business

Perhaps the most crucial thing you need to keep in mind when thinking about online review sites such as Yelp.com is that they operate on the presumption of being totally impartial. In a fair, transparent world, the best businesses would get the best ratings and reviews and would grow thanks to them, while poorer businesses would receive worse ratings and critical reviews and would see their profits decline.

But despite the supposed impartiality of Yelp.com and despite the fact that the site's mission is a noble one... those reviews and ratings? Those are all left by human beings and, unfortunately, just as humans can be kind, honest, and generous, we can also be fickle, vindictive, and misleading. It's as true in romance as it is in Yelping!

To help you best navigate the complex and ever-changing landscape that is Yelp.com (and believe me, it is ever changing, with reviews popping up and disappearing in a never ending cycle and user impressions spreading like wildfire), this book is broken up into focused, helpful chapters. I recommend you read the whole thing, of course, to get the whole picture, but you can always refer back to specific sections later on down the road, as some parts will be more or less relevant to you and your business.

When you have finished the book, you will have learned a cautionary tale or two, you will have heard of some Yelp.com success stories, you'll know more of the terms and slang Yelpers use, and you will have your road map/answer key to help you get more of those good comments, avoid the bad stuff, and get as much of the ugly offline as fast as possible!

Yelp.com can help a business put its best foot forward, or it can muddy the reputation of even the finest establishment. In either case, though, you can have a big impact on the way Yelp impacts you, as long as you know what steps to take. The only step you can't afford to take is none: like it or not, the Yelpers are here, and they are Yelping away!

YelpSpeak – Let's Talk the Talk

A teacher would call it "the language of the discipline." A researcher might call this a Glossary of Terms. Maybe it's the lexicon, or perhaps the vernacular.

I'm just going to call it… YelpSpeak.

Before we dive into the meat of the issue, before we rant and rave against the notorious Yelp filter, or praise the businesses that have managed to stay afloat even with the anchor of a YelpFuck trying to drag them down, I'm going to lay out some of the terms you'll find that people use when talking about Yelp.

I probably should have mentioned this earlier, and you probably already figured it out, but they're not all pretty. Why? Because like we said, when it comes to Yelp.com, there's good, there's bad, and there is most certainly ugly.

This list is somewhat abbreviated, and the terms on it are not "official" in any sense, but as you trawl the World Wide Web, you might spot them on popular sites like UrbanDictionary.com (we thank them for some of the very terms below, in fact!) just as soon as you'll see them on Yelp.com itself. And you will certainly see this language used on social networking sites like Facebook and Twitter.

In short, when people talk about Yelp, this is some of the YelpSpeak they use to do it.

RATING: They can be anywhere from one star to five, with one being the Kiss of Death, ad five being the Waters of Life, if you'll that much metaphor in one sentence.

REVIEW: This is the actual writing that a user leaves behind beyond the simple rating. Yelp reviews can swell your business or they can dry it up.

TROLL: The internet troll and the more specific Yelp troll is a strange, angry subset: these are people whose only goal is to provoke others, most always through wildly negative, lurid commentary. The worst thing about a Yelp troll is that in many to most cases, they will not even have visited the business or tried the service they are attacking, so preventing bad ratings and reviews from them requires careful monitoring of Yelp.com – merely running an exemplary business is no longer enough!

YELPER/YELPIE: This is your typical Yelp user/enthusiast. This is the group you need to appeal to on Yelp, and the group that is helping to screw you over if you don't. Fortunately, you'll soon know how to handle them!

YELP CASUALTY: This is an important one because if you're reading this book, it's likely you may be a Yelp casualty. A Yelp casualty is a business that significantly loses business because of an undeservingly low overall rating due to just one or two reviews.

YELP DOUCHE: Yes, people do say this. The Yelp Douche is one who vents anger and frustration against a business while hiding behind a veil of anonymity. An upset customer who leaves a bad review is one thing; a douchebag who is just generally upset is something else.

YELP EFFECT: When the popularity of a given store/eatery/etc. surges based on no apparent reason other than a series of positive Yelp reviews and ratings, the Yelp Effect is in full effect. It is a sort of hysteria/psychosis, and it can be either great boon or burden.

YELP ELITE: I'll let Yelp handle this one itself: *"The Yelp Elite Squad is our way of recognizing and rewarding yelpers who are active evangelists and role models, both on and off the site. Elite-worthiness is based on a number of things, including well-written reviews, great tips on mobile, a fleshed-out personal profile, an active voting and complimenting record, and playing nice with others. Members of the Elite Squad are designated by a shiny Elite badge on their account profile."*

YELP-FU: This one comes with thanks to UrbanDictionary.com – Yelp-Fu is the rarely-subtle "art" of using choice words and phrases to unfairly cut a business down. It is a review using words like "terrible customer service" or "no atmosphere" or the like, when in fact a simple, specific, and constructive comment is what the experience warranted.

YELP FUCK: You don't need to use your imagination on this one. It is an act not of reviewing a business, but of attacking a business via Yelp.

YELP-O-MANIAC: The Yelp-o-Maniac (or YelpManiac, for short) has multiple Yelp accounts, and uses all of them to both bolster statements that have made, creating the illusion of online popularity and clout, and to attack others users and businesses plural times over, creating the illusion that they are not just one disgruntled loser.

What (the Hell) is Yelp All About, Anyway?

For you experienced Yelpers out there, this chapter might be nothing but a review of information you already know. I thought it might be helpful to offer a quick bit of history about Yelp.com, a sort of corporate bio that would help the business owner understand more about Yelp's business model and foundation.

In short, this chapter will help the uninitiated understand the "What" of Yelp.com. But I bet some of the statistics we've dug up will surprise even the more experienced Yelp users out there! And you will certainly gain a better sense of context.

Yelp.com is a ratings and review aggregator that allows prospective customers to learn about businesses, products, and services based off the experiences others have had there. That is about as simply stated as possible. Yelp is not the only website around, but it is far and away the biggest fish in that pond. CitySearch and Yahoo! Local and other such sites offer many of the same functions as Yelp and rely on a similar interface platform, but for sheer market penetration, none comes close to Yelp. But you already knew that, that's why you're reading this book!

How did Yelp get so big (and powerful)? The "origin story" of Yelp is simple enough. Apparently, co-founder Jeremy Stoppelman was having difficulty finding a good doctor in his new hometown of San Francisco, CA, and relayed his wish that some services existed that would make it easy to find a reliable, well-liked MD to his associate, Russel Simmons. The idea for Yelp.com was born that day in the autumn of 2004. And it was pitched to investor Max Levchin (of PayPal.com fame) later that day. By that evening, the idea was funded with one million dollars of seed money. Within a few weeks, the fledgling site was launched.

And by mid-2005, the site was growing like a weed! Thanks to its own success, and thanks to multiple huge cash infusions from venture capitalists, Yelp is now one of the most highly trafficked sites in the world.

The brilliance behind Yelp.com is that its content is both user-generated and user-oriented. People just like you and me provide all the major content for the site, and we are also its consumers. In theory, then, Yelp should represent the ultimate form of democratic decision-making. In practice, though, there is often a corporate hand driving traffic to certain businesses and away from others. This is done by influencing which reviews are promoted and widely seen, thus having a positive effect on a business's ratings, and by influencing which reviews and ratings will be buried, rarely read and with no potential for positive influence on an establishment's rating… and therefore costing it money! More on that in later chapters, for now let's stay focused on the basics.

The next chapter will feature a brief "walk-through" of how a user creates a Yelp account and starts leaving reviews and ratings. It will also take you through how a business owner creates his or her business's Yelp page, or "claims" a business page someone else has created about them.

(Yeah, you read that right: anyone can create a Yelp page about your business, so the chances are good that your business is already "on" Yelp even if you have never even once been to the site before! And that means the chances are great that your establishment is currently being misrepresented in everything from the most accurate phone/address to what kind of business you even operate! Don't worry: you'll soon know how to take ownership of your own online presence!)

Let's take the rest of this chapter to talk about some stats that should once and for all convince you that Yelp.com is a force to be reckoned with, and one you can't afford to ignore.

- **For each of the first months of the year 2013, Yelp.com received over 100 million unique visitors.** That means an average of 3.3 million people on Yelp every single day. That's a lot of potential eyes on your business, no?

- **To date, there are just under 40 million reviews on Yelp.com.** Any one of those, or even many hundreds of them, could be about your find business, drawing in traffic both from Yelp itself and increasing your overall presence on the web thanks to some "free SEM," or Search Engine Marketing.

- **Retail and restaurants account for about 45% of Yelp.com's content.** So of you own or operate a business selling anything from toys to pool supplies to sandwiches, you had better "own" your presence on Yelp.com!

- **Every additional star in a Yelp review Leads to around a 7.5% increase in a business's revenue!** That means that with a few great ratings that bump you up to four or five stars, you could see thousands and thousands more dollars in business from month to month, or even week to week!

- **Customer Service is king!** Studies have shown that people who report good customer service routinely leave 5-star reviews, while those who leave comments about poor customer service usually leave only a single star.

And one more little factoid to get you thinking about the juggernaut that is Yelp.com...

• **Yelp's IPO (or Initial Public Offering) was on March 2, 2012 and its shares were valued at fifteen dollars a piace, giving the company a value of around 900 million dollars. Within that first day of trading, shares were up to more than $24 a piece, an increase of more than 60%... an increase that made it a billion dollar company in a single day!***

(Note: these statistics are the latest available at the time of writing, and are taken from Yelp.com itself in good faith, unless otherwise noted.)

(*http://money.cnn.com/2012/03/02/technology/yelp_ipo/)

How to Use Yelp.com – The Basics

By the time you have finished reading this chapter, you will understand how to tackle many of the basic, core things one must understand to get the most out of Yelp. And to minimize the damage Yelp can do to their business, of course. (That two-headed coin is sort of the recurring theme when it comes to Yelp.com, no?)

To make the most of this section, I'd recommend you have the book either laid out on the desk beside you or loaded on your iPad or eReader and have Yelp.com open on your computer, especially if you are new to the whole Yelp thing. For those who already have some experience with the site, this chapter can be more of a refresher.

Now, without further ado, let's do it!

How to Create a Yelp.com Account (User/Reviewer)

This process is blissfully simple, don't worry. (And it may not even apply to you if you are a business owner/manager, but it can be good to have a personal Yelp page even so: as a regular old Yelper, you can look at your own business's page more objectively, and you can study the pages and reviews of other businesses, learning what seems to be working for them and what seems to be a mess!)

- Go to Yelp.com
- Click "SIGN UP" at the top of the page
- Enter your information (you may be able to/prompted to sign up using your Facebook profile, but note that you can elect to bypass that option if you don't use or don't want to use a Facebook account)

- You will get an email confirming your account – follow the steps in that email and… you're done! Your Yelp account is set up, and you are an official Yelper!

Making the Most of Your Yelp Account

So now you have a Yelp account. Well done. But there's more, of course. What you have just done is created the most bare-bones type of Yelp.com user account. In order to make the most of your Yelp experience, you need to take additional steps.

By filling out all the details of your profile page and by becoming a trusted, regular Yelp user, you will gain more "power" on Yelp.com, with your reviews more heavily weighed and carrying more influence. The goal (assuming you're really into Yelp) is to become a member of the "Yelp Elite Squad." We'll let the Yelp.com FAQ page handle that one directly:

"The Yelp Elite Squad is our way of recognizing and rewarding yelpers who are active evangelists and role models, both on and off the site. Elite-worthiness is based on a number of things, including well-written reviews, great tips on mobile, a fleshed-out personal profile, an active voting and complimenting record, and playing nice with others. Members of the Elite Squad are designated by a shiny Elite badge on their account profile."

Whether or not you become a member of the Elite Squad, you definitely want to have its members on your side, writing you great reviews and leaving 5-star ratings, so it is a good idea for you to understand how they came by that "shiny Elite badge."

Frustrated with yelp!

To enhance your status and clout on Yelp.com, follow these steps.

Edit/Complete your "Public Profile"

> • Sign in, then click "edit your profile" under your username (top right of the screen)

> • Fill in all the basic data you wish, such as your Nickname, your Hometown, your "Headline" and so on. A balance between privacy and what info you choose to put online is always tricky to manage, but for the record, the more complete your profile, the more clout it carries on Yelp. (Note: not everything has be entirely about you, exactly…)

> • Add "Friends." Find your friends on Yelp or reach out to new people. The more friends you have on Yelp, the more clout.

> • Add Locations. While you don't want to overdo it with Locations, featuring one Primary Location and two or three secondary places (a location means something like "New York City" or "Tampa, FL" for the record) you increase your credibility when reviewing things in those areas.

> • Now start writing reviews and leaving ratings! The more you do this, the more influence you will carry. Even if your account was established just as a learning tool for yourself, you should write a handful of reviews to put yourself in the shoes of those who might be reviewing you someday soon. Just think of places you already know, love, and frequent if you don't feel like going out and trying someplace new.

Listing A (Your) Business on Yelp

You might find this step easy. Strangely easy, in fact: even if you have never been on Yelp.com before, there is a good chance your business is already listed there. A business can end up on Yelp.com in one of three primary ways:

- A business owner/manager elects to "Add a Business" directly
- Users have added a business
- Yelp has added a business using info it gets from other parties, such as Google or the Yellow Pages or from public records

Setting-up a Business Account

Ultimately, *how* your business got listed on Yelp.com is not what matters. It's the accuracy of the information displayed on the site that means business, or the lack thereof!

You can claim your business's Yelp profile simply by following the steps outlined after you click "Create Your Free Account" on the page **biz.yelp.com**

And here's why you had better take the time to do it...

If a customer tries a phone number or website they see on Yelp and finds it to be out of date, your business has fallen off the face of the earth on their minds. Think of the implication of that: say you spent thousands of dollars a few years back to had a totally new website designed, new phones installed—the works! If your Yelp listing is from before that change, your sleek website and 1-800 number means nothing to thousands of potential customers, because they'll never know about them!

Once you have set up your business account, go through these steps:

- Check all the information listed about your business, or make sure to submit it all correctly if you are adding your business. Check the address, the contact info, your hours, your website, all of it!
- Add a few pictures of your business and/or your products. If you choose some pictures and put them on Yelp, you maximize the chance that people will see favorable images of your business. If you don't add pictures, the only ones on the site might be negative.
- Create a "Yelp Deal." These allow you to offer your current and prospective customers deals they can only get on Yelp.

Now here's the catch: some of the most crucial information, such as Pricing (as indicated by $$ symbols) and your establishment's attire? You can't change that stuff! That info is dictated by customers. It can change over time, but only as influenced by Yelp users, not by business owners. So monitor your page, and know that the only way you may be able to influence some of the key factors is to patiently create the environment you want to see expressed online.

With your Yelp Business Account, you can also track various metrics that will show you who is visiting your page and how long they seem to spend clicking around on it; valuable information as you keep updated and editing your Yelp page!

But the most important thing a business owner can do on Yelp, though, is to…

Engage with Your Customers!

Having positive interactions with your customers is far and away the best way to increase your business's standing on Yelp and, ultimately, to help your profits. This topic is a big one, so it gets its own chapter a bit later on in the book.

How to Generate a Yelp Ad

Just like anywhere else on the internet, not to mention the rest of the world at large, sometimes you have to do some self-promotion on Yelp. And just like usual with Yelp.com, there is also a rather sinister motivator for a local business to place an ad on Yelp:

Until you pay for advertising that will go on your Yelp business page, your competitors will be getting free advertising in the space that should be yours! It's true. And truly frustrating.

Let's let Yelp.com speak for itself. When you pay for "Targeted Local Advertising" on Yelp, here are the three main "benefits" you can expect:

- *Advertise on Yelp Search -* **Yelp Ads are placed on search result pages, so that users searching in your area will see your business above Yelp's natural search results.**

- *Advertise on Related Businesses –* **Ads are also placed on the business pages of nearby businesses in your category.**

- *Removal of Competitor Ads –* **Advertising on Yelp will remove competitor ads from your Yelp business page, allowing you to keep the purchasing focus on your business.**

Is it a bit crazy that you have to pay for ads in order to not have others' ads on your own business's page? We'll leave that decision to you. If you want to go ahead and face the music, though, do it by other clicking "Advertise" at the bottom of the homepage or by just typing **Yelp.com/advertise**, and you'll be directed along from there.

Yelp Gift Certificates and Deals

Everyone loves gift certificates. Your Yelp followers will too. Why? Because what could be an easier gift than cash made to seem thoughtful!

Yelp gift certificates are 1 for 1, so when someone spends $100 on a gift certificate and sends it to a friend, that friend gets a $100 certificate to your business. The incentive behind them for the customer is just the same as any "traditional" gift certificate. The incentive for you is the near-guarantee that someone who gets a gift certificate to your establishment will come in and give you a try, surely falling in love with your place.

Yelp Deals are going to cost you a bit more, but may lead to repeat customers who would otherwise not have tried your business. In a Yelp Deal, you offer a given amount of credit at your establishment for a lower dollar price, so for example $20 cash could buy $30 worth of credit to your store.

The biggest drawback to these two otherwise standard marketing initiatives? For a Yelp gift certificate, Yelp takes 10% of the fee. For a Yelp Deal, they take 30%. Pretty high mark up for processing that is handled almost entirely by computer? Yes. Is it worth the fees? Worth a try maybe… you decide.

The Hated Filter

As we have discussed at some length (OK, perhaps a "dead horse" metaphor would be allowed), the driving principle behind Yelp.com is objectivity. For the model they have created to remain both fair and reliable, it has to be totally unbiased; there must be no way for a business's Yelp reviews or ratings to be influenced other than by the feedback and ratings left by actual people who have had actual experiences.

But we all know that's not the way things are. Which sucks, but it's true, so let's talk about the way things are in the real world of Yelp.com. For the sake of staying focused on the topic at hand, I'm not going to bother talking about the corrupting influence, both negative and positive, created by people motivated to sabotage a given business or falsely inflate another through artificial reviews and ratings. Today, it's all about The Filter.

What is this Yelp Filter that People Always Clamor About?

The Yelp filter is an "algorithmic processes" that analyzes the "quality" of a given review and reviewer based on plural metrics and attributes. The filter factors in attributes of both the content of a given review and based on the person creating it. The word "quality" in this context can be taken to mean, essentially, the reliability of the review and reviewer; the trustworthiness... as perceived by Yelp.

But there is a tricky double-standard at work: as the reliability of a given review is largely based on how Yelp feels about a given reviewer, you can't leave reviews that will have any real impact until you have already left many reviews… that have impact!

What is the Dividing Line Between What Gets Filtered and What Gets Featured?

(We have already talked about how you create and flesh-out a Yelp account – make sure to re-visit that section of Chapter 4 for clarification on what constitutes a robust, established Yelper.)

Someone who has been on Yelp for years and is well "established" (most of the words in quotation marks are the lingo used by Yelp.com itself, by the way) is going to get the benefit of the doubt when writing reviews about most any establishment.

Yelp.com's official blog has a section that reads:

"It's tough for an algorithm to tell the difference between a business owner aggressively putting a laptop in front of a client and saying, "Give me 5 stars!" and that same business owner flipping the laptop around and manufacturing a fake 5-star review about themselves."

But what about a customer who had a great experience and then writes an honest, effusive review? Why is their high praise about a fine experience likely to be relegated to the virtual dust bin? Because the Yelp Filter doesn't care about your honest experience, it cares about your devotion to Yelp.

Let's be very clear about what is going on here, and draw a distinction between a person we will call "You" and a person we will call "Established Yelper" by creating a little scenario:

You go to a pharmacy and have your prescription filled. The process is quick, simple, and pleasant. In fact, it is so pleasant you decide to let the world know about it: on returning home, you create a Yelp account and you leave the pharmacy a pleasant review and a 5-star rating! It is your first ever Yelp experience, and it tops off the pleasant day you have just had. Until you realize that your review is nowhere to be seen on Yelp.com's main pages, and in fact you have to go digging through a "Filtered Reviews" section to locate it. Your review will be seen by almost no one and your rating is not helping the pharmacy that helped you. You... have been filtered out.

Now for the Established Yelper's turn...

The Established Yelper goes to the pharmacy one evening and finds a long line there. After waiting in it, they are impatient and testy, and they leave in a foul mood, angry at the pharmacy for being busy at the hour when they arrived. It seems to them that ineffectual service was the culprit for the delay, not the fact that it was just after work hours, so they dash off a quick 2-star yelp review riddled with complaints about the pharmacy. Because they are an Established Yelper, the world will see their poor review.

You and the Established Yelper both went to the same pharmacy. You had different experiences and you wrote about them honestly, at least as much as possible given the subjective nature of human emotion. But your good experience, so positive you decided to join Yelp just to share it, has been rendered invisible, while the negative experience of the Established Yelper is front and center.

It's like Yelp's filter is saying: "Sorry you only wanted to comment on your positive experience with one business, but we don't much listen to folks who don't review a few dozen places first."

Fair? Hell no. But there it is.

They can claim the filter itself is objective with relative impunity, but here's the catch: who programmed the algorithm upon which it operates? Not an objective program, but rather a person working for Yelp.

A Cautionary Tale

For a company with such a positive, civic-minded aura around it, Yelp.com sure does get slapped with a lot of lawsuits. And the primary charges frequently leveled against Yelp are not pretty: extortion, fraudulent practices, and libel/slander.

In 2010, one lawsuit involved no fewer than nine small businesses banding together to bring charges of defamation against the growing juggernaut review site. And there was a similar suit alleging extortion the following year. And several were filed in 2012.

In fact, there has been so much legal action taken against Yelp.com that I'm not going to bother with a laundry list of all the cases; instead I'm going to focus on one specific small businessperson's experiences. His Yelp saga spans the gamut from first trying to establish an amicable relationship with the company and, when that failed, deciding instead to go to war.

Yelp.com has beaten just about every one of the legal challenges it has faced in the past. After all, it is a site that aggregates content from its users, and is not actually authoring any of the material which has incensed the people who sued, right? Well, that might be only technically true. Which could also be interpreted at as being… false.

Let's take a step back…

Dr. Mal Braverman is a dentist held in the fine standing among the dental community. He is a one of the founders of the New York chapter of the American Academy of Cosmetic Dentistry, and has served as that institution's president. Dr. Braverman is a fellow at the International Academy of Dental-Facial Esthetics and one of two dentists in New York City who is listed in the Castle & Connolly Publication *America's Cosmetic Doctors & Dentists*. He was also featured in New York Magazine's "Best Beauty Docs" issue, which focused on New York's top plastic surgeons, dermatologists, and cosmetic dentists. Braverman is well-known in New York as the smile makeover dentist for the Maury Povich show.

But according to Yelp.com… he sucks.

Or at least that is what you would think were you to come across his practice, Smile Studio, on Yelp.com. Dr. Braverman has three reviews, all of them scathing, and all of them featuring that damning 1-star rating.

Featured prominently on Dr. Braverman's page? Ads for other dentists – competitors – who are just a few miles away from Smile Studio's offices. These are paid ads, of course.

However, if one bothers to take the time to go to Dr. Braverman / Smile Studio's filtered reviews, and for the record, that means finding a the words "Filtered Reviews" which are written in a tiny font size and pale gray in color, and even making that link work requires the discouraging use of "captcha," one gets a wildly different picture!

Yelp has filtered out more than two dozen glowing reviews of Dr. Mal Braverman and his Smile Studio practice. The ratings reviewers have left are almost all 5-stars. And many of the reviews were left by people extolling the treatment they have gotten from Braverman over many, many years!

So according to Yelp.com's filtered reviews… he's great.

Three vitriolic, negative reviews with terrible ratings, unfiltered, and affecting a doctor's livelihood, versus almost thirty positive reviews with great ratings, all but hidden from the world.

Those are the basic facts. And if that were the end of the story, one could rail against Yelp for its obviously flawed filter, and one could fairly say they were unfairly damaging this man's reputation, but what no one could say is that Yelp was engaging in anything outside of the law or, frankly, even anything out of line with their own stated, self-imposed guidelines and practices.

But the story doesn't end there; in fact it's just beginning.

After seeing that he had received several cutting reviews and terrible ratings on Yelp.com, and after realizing that he had plural good reviews that had been filtered out, Dr. Braverman did the logical thing, and contacted the company. Or rather, he tried to contact the company – you can't ever really get an employee of Yelp's main offices on the phone. Instead you get in touch with sales representatives (that is, when they haven't proactively reached out to you, trying to convince you to buy Yelp ads, which often start around $300 a month).

Dr. Braverman expressed his concerns and frustrations to the Yelp salesperson he reached, and was told that there was nothing at all Yelp could do about the prominence of his bad reviews and the obscurity of all the good ones. That selection process was all up to the objective, omniscient filter. *But…* said the sales rep… perhaps is Dr. Braverman would be willing to purchase some advertising space from Yelp, they could at least perhaps just maybe make one or two good reviews avoid that awful filter. And maybe some of the bad reviews would go away after all, if he bought ad space.

If that sounds vaguely like extortion, then you are in tune. At least, as part of the thrust of Dr. Braverman's suit alleges. To quote the doctor:

"Yelp has an algorithm with is surreptitiously despicable, which unfairly defames [dental] practices, hurting their reputations and seriously affecting their incomes from traffic from the internet, all for [Yelp.com's] own advantage, seeking increased profit for their business."

It remains to be seen if Yelp is violating the letter of the law or merely the spirit when it comes to soliciting ad space in an extortive manner.

Where there is less gray area is in the arena of defamation. Yelp hides behind the assertion that they don't write any of the material that appears in their reviews, and that they don't leave ratings. But it is not hard to argue that in an editorial capacity, they have at least some degree of authorship over the damning portrait they have created of Dr. Braverman and Smile Studio. If indeed their filter was certifiably objective, then there would be essentially no grounds for a case (or at least only shaky ground, at best). But if indeed Yelp sales representatives intimate that the purchase of ads could affect the reviews and ratings displayed about a given business, then the algorithm behind the filter is not an independent, isolated decision-maker about which the company can do nothing but wring its hands.

To put it bluntly, if there is anything a Yelp.com employee can that effects the reviews and ratings on display about any given business, they are engaged in a type of censorship/authorship, and likely guilty of defamation.

To put it simply, consider this sentence:
"He is not a bad person."
Clear cut, right? No ambiguity, right?
Now let's remove one of the words…
"He is __ a bad person."

And there we have it! By removing one sixth of the content of that sentence from view, we have totally changed what is being said! Now, as stated, this is a simplistic example, and not a direct comparison to what happened to Dr. Braverman (and many others) when certain content was obscured and other content displayed, but if I may be so humble…

It is not a bad illustration.

Some Tips on Hacking Yelp.com

Let me clear the airwaves before we get started with this chapter: the term hack is used here to mean something positive, not anything pejorative, and certainly nothing involving illegal activity, either with a computer or with a hatchet. "Hack" has taken on a meaning akin to finding "a clever solution to a tricky problem" (thank you UrbanDictionary.com).

By this point in the book, you probably have a good sense of what Yelp.com is all about and you are comfortable with the basics of setting up a Yelp page for your business, modifying the information on your page, tracking your ratings and reviews, and so on. We have also talked about a lot of the pitfalls and pain that can be caused by bad Yelp reviews, we've talked about that damned filter, and we have looked at some specific tales of Yelp.com-related woe.

But guess what? It's not all doom and gloom—there is indeed good that can come to you and your business thanks to Yelp.com. But to really use the site, to not only have Yelp not screw you over, but to in fact have it increase your positive profile with the public and ultimately drive customer traffic and sales to you, you need to know how to do more than just edit your business's address information, and you need to do more than just hope more good reviews than bad roll in.

In fact, even good reviews from satisfied customers merit your taking action to leverage them the same way as bad reviews call for intervention and mitigation. If you want to do more than merely survive on Yelp.com, if you want your business to even, dare I say, thrive there, you are going to want to follow as many of these tips as possible!

Respond to Your Reviews

The Bad New First...

If you just got a scathing, blistering review posted on your Yelp page – and I mean a real rant filled with rage over your awful service, your terrible products, and the horrible decorations in your men's room – take a deep breath. Don't take it personally; it's about your business, not you as a person. And believe it or not, this bad review might present you an opportunity.

As many people who see the bad reviews you get on Yelp will likely see the responses you leave in reply to them. This is your chance to show that your business is receptive, responsive, and sensitive to a customer's wants and needs. If you can address the specific issues raised in a complaint, those seeing the review/response exchange will likely be left with an impression of how a problem was solved, not how a problem occurred in the first place.

And the Good News...

If you just got a laudatory, enraptured review, a 5-star celebration of your business, your products, your staff, and on and on, respond to it! Say thank you! Hell, say: "Thank you so very much! We appreciate you taking the time to come in and the time you took to leave such a nice review!"

People will see how appreciative you are, and that will encourage them to patronize your business. It will also encourage them to leave a review of their own because, let's face it, people like to be praised.

Here's a catch: while a kind response to a great rating and review might help you get more reviews, you should never directly ask for anyone to leave a review, at least according to the folks at Yelp.com. The logic here is that by asking someone to leave a review, you have robbed any review they leave of its organic, spontaneous nature, and it is more likely to sound canned and, therefore, more likely to be filtered.

Promote Your Yelp Page Subtly

Instead of directly asking for reviews, which we'll take for granted as a bad practice, why not just make it super easy for people to find their way to your business on Yelp?

How? Easy! Just place a Yelp link/widget prominently on your website, or even in your email's signature text. Anywhere people are likely to see your business while on their computers or mobile devices might be a good place for a link or clickable icon.

And definitely try to get your hands on one of those nifty People Love Us on Yelp.com window clings or stickers. It will help keep Yelp on people's minds if they see the sticker and actively associate it with the fine service and products they are in the process of enjoying thanks to your business. If you can't get a "legitimate" sticker or window cling, who is to stop you from printing your own? Certainly not I…

A Picture is Worth…

OK, maybe a picture on Yelp is not worth a thousand words, and surely it's not worth a thousand great reviews and 5-star ratings, but pictures are incredibly important for your business's presence on Yelp.com!

You need to make sure you have enough appropriate images, but also don't go overboard: too large of a gallery, and a viewer's eyes will start to glaze over. I don't have a magic number to recommend, but somewhere around ten good images has seemed to be the sweet spot in all my research Yelping experience. And be logical about it: a restaurant needs to show its classy interior, some happy diners, and a dish or two; an auto body shop needs to show some great-looking automobiles! And make sure to include the best possible picture you can of the front of your business so people can find it more easily, too!

And here is something that's also key for you to note is that the absence of pictures will send up a huge red flag: if people come to your business's Yelp page and see no pictures, it makes the business seem less appealing, less approachable, and even less "real." So if you don't have good pictures of your business, take some or have someone else do it, don't skip this step!

Let's Make a Deal

A Yelp deal, that is! Go back to Chapter 4 and re-read it twice if you don't remember what these are!

Make Direct Contact

Yelp.com let's its users send direct messages to one another (this applies to a business-to-customer message as well), and taking the time to reach out to both your fans and detractors is a great way to strengthen the relationship with the former and repair it with the latter. It is hard for a customer to stay angry – or at least *as* angry – with a business that takes the time to directly contact them, and I mean beyond just responding to a review.

A message should be a new, original communication directed right to an individual and addressing either a specific complaint or, more happily, a specific compliment. My experience has shown me that taking this action results in soothing the ire of the irate, and in inspiring the already happy supporter to go a step beyond, sharing not only their original good experience, but also letting the world know how you went out of your way to reach out to them, because you are a great business (you clever dog).

Wrapping it All Up

So that's it, then! You are now poised to grow your business exponentially thanks to your total mastery of all that is Yelp.com... right?

Well... OK, maybe it's not that easy. And frankly, your experience with Yelp may be everything from a wild increase in your business's popularity and success or it may be a constant damage control patrol. The waters that are Yelp.com remain largely uncharted even for those who have spent a long time sailing them, because the content – those ratings and reviews – come from other people, and you just can't perfectly predict what those people will do!

Here's one thing you can be certain of, though: the more time you spend on Yelp, and the more you interact with people on the site, both well-wishers and detractors, the better your business will do in the long run. The single best thing you can have on Yelp.com is a long, rich history. Businesses that have been featured on the site for years and that have received dozens and dozens of reviews are more likely to be seen as more trustworthy than newcomers, and it's just that simple.

So if you are already active on Yelp, good for you – keep at it! If not, hurry, it's not too late! You can start to build your Yelp brand any time, just know that it might be a while before your effort pay off.

As I said earlier, though, the one thing that might be worse than a scathing review and terrible rating from an irate customer, is to not exist on Yelp at all. Anymore, if your business does not have a presence on Yelp.com, it's almost as if you've put the "Closed" sign in your window and headed on home.

So whether you love Yelp or hate it with a passion, you still need to play ball. You should now have all the basics in your tool chest. The rest is up to you.

Check your information regularly and make sure everything from your phone number to your hours of operation are listed correctly.

Interact with the people who take the time to review and comment about you.

Post some great pictures.

And remember: don't take the bad stuff personally... it's just the way things are sometimes in the world of Yelp.com.

Made in the USA
Las Vegas, NV
16 December 2023

83022750R00024